THE CITY WE BUILT

BLACK LEADERS OF AUSTIN

Published by Arcadia Children's Books,
A division of Arcadia Publishing, Inc.
Charleston, South Carolina
www.arcadiapublishing.com

Designed by Jessica Nevins

ISBN 978-1-4671-9722-9

Library of Congress Control Number: 2023951126

Printed in China

THE CITY WE BUILT

BLACK LEADERS OF AUSTIN

Illustrated by **Sadé Lawson**

Written by **Terry P. Mitchell**
and **Carre Adams**

Produced in partnership with the Black Leaders Collective and the
George Washington Carver Museum, Cultural and Genealogy Center

arcadia
CHILDREN'S BOOKS

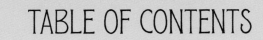

TABLE OF CONTENTS

INTRODUCTION

My daughter and I bond a lot over reading historical children's books. We enjoy learning about changemakers from our past; courageous men and women who've made a positive difference in the world around them. But quite often, I notice that the leaders recognized in so many books for children are bigger, more global figures, rather than the local heroes and legends who make their cities great.

When I founded the Black Leaders Collective (BLC), I became especially curious about our local history and the impact Black leaders who came before us had had on the city of Austin. I quickly realized there was little archived documentation about these key figures. I brought the idea to BLC as a way of preserving our history, recognizing our ancestors of leadership, and telling the world our stories. The concept grew bigger and bigger when I introduced the idea to Carre Adams, chief curator and director of the George Washington Carver Museum, Cultural and Genealogy Center, as well as the rest of our BLC collaborators. And once we got Sadé Lawson involved with illustrations, magic started to kick up! Before long, a small

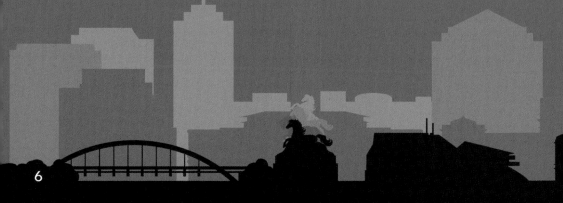

vision became a big, beautiful reality: the book you're holding in your hands right now.

Within these inspiring and gorgeously illustrated pages, I want young readers to become aware of the hidden figures who have been the backbone of our beloved city, despite very little recognition. I want them to honor those who came before us, and to see themselves as the next generation of changemakers in the pursuit of justice for all. We should all understand that we each have a significant part to play in the fight for love and equity, and that sometimes, small acts turn into major movements, if only we—like the remarkable Black leaders who helped build our city—dare to be courageous.

All love,

Terry Mitchell

ADA ANDERSON

An influential Civil Rights activist, educator, and arts advocate, **Ada Anderson** (1921–2021) achieved many remarkable firsts! Born in 1921, Ada would go on to become the first African American to enroll in the University of Texas Master of Library Science program. She was the first Black woman on a bank board in Austin and the first African American elected to the Austin Community College Board. In 1953, she helped start the Austin chapter of Jack and Jill of America, dedicated to nurturing future Black leaders and supporting children in the community.

But Ada's pioneering spirit didn't end there. She also founded the Austin Human Relations Commission, working to make Austin's schools, hotels, and businesses open to everyone. She taught at Austin Community College and UT, served on the board of the Laguna Gloria Art Museum, and received numerous accolades, including induction into the Texas Black Women's Hall of Fame and the African American Women's Hall of Fame.

Her passion for the arts led her to cofound the Austin Lyric Opera and establish the Leadership Enrichment Arts Program, introducing the arts to low-income and minority youth. Recognized as Woman of the Year by the Women's Symphony League of Austin in 1992 and honored by the Texas House of Representatives in 2005, Ada Anderson's dedication continues to inspire future Black leaders of Austin to this day!

ADA DEBLANC SIMOND

Ada DeBlanc Simond (1903–1989) was a living legend for her tireless efforts to educate and help the people of Austin. Born in Louisiana, Ada moved to Austin when she was eleven. She left school to help raise her siblings and take jobs. But she always tried to continue her education.

While raising her own children, Ada worked at various schools, often taking free classes for payment. Over time, she earned degrees in family life education, child development, and home economics, and she became the head of the Home Economics department at Tillotson College (now Huston-Tillotson University).

Starting in 1942, Ada worked at the Texas Tuberculosis Association. She traveled across Texas educating poor families about health, nutrition, and medical services, while also setting up community health organizations. In 1967, Ada went on to work or volunteer at state and local departments of health, churches, and local organizations that helped the poor and elderly.

After 1977, Ada switched to a career as a historian and writer. She published books for children (including a series about Black Austin families living in the early 1900s), and wrote articles for local papers. She also cofounded the George Washington Carver Museum.

In 1986, Ada was inducted into the Texas Women's Hall of Fame. She died at 85, in 1989.

AZIE TAYLOR MORTON

Azie Taylor Morton (1936–2003) served as treasurer of the United States from 1977 to 1981, while Jimmy Carter was president. She remains the only African American to ever hold that office.

Azie was born in the farming community of Dale, Texas, on February 1, 1936. She was smart and worked hard in school, graduating at the top of her class from Huston–Tillotson College (now Huston-Tillotson University) in Austin.

Before becoming treasurer, Azie served on President John F. Kennedy's Committee on Equal Employment Opportunity, which worked to help people of color get fair treatment from employers. From 1972 to 1976, she was a special assistant to Robert Schwarz Strauss, the chair of the Democratic National Committee. She was also an election observer for the presidential elections in other countries, including Haiti, Senegal, and the Dominican Republic.

She worked hard—in the United States and around the world—to expand rights and opportunities for Black people of all nationalities.

Did you know? During the time Azie was treasurer of the United States, her signature was printed on US currency!

COUNCILMAN
BERL L. HANDCOX

BERL HANDCOX

Berl Handcox (1932–2020) grew up in Denton, Texas, and Wichita, Kansas. He served in the US Navy during the Korean War on the aircraft carrier USS *Valley Forge*. After his service, he earned a degree at Prairie View A&M College, and went on to become a teacher and coach.

In the late 1960s, Berl and his family moved to Austin, and Berl worked at the IBM corporation, training workers. He was promoted to Equal Employment Opportunity Coordinator, becoming one of the highest ranking Black employees at IBM.

Berl was very aware of the disadvantages of Black families in Austin—especially in East Austin, where city improvements often lagged. In 1971, he won a seat on the Austin City Council—the first Black council member since the 1870s. He focused on improving the lives of the Black communities in East Austin. He initiated the Community Improvement Program (also known as the Handcox Paving Plan) to fix East Austin's roads. He also initiated plans to improve and modernize water treatment plants—starting in East Austin.

Berl was a beloved community member, and his work impacted families throughout Austin. Before his death in 2020, a water treatment plant was named in his honor.

BERTHA SADLER MEANS

Bertha Sadler Means (1920–2021) was known and loved for being a businesswoman, teacher, Civil Rights activist, and founder of the Mothers Action Council, which helped integrate Austin's public facilities during the 1960s.

Born near Valley Mills, Texas, Bertha went to school in Waco and earned degrees from Huston-Tillotson College (now Huston-Tillotson University) and University of Texas Austin. She was a teacher in the Austin Independent School District and also at Austin-area colleges and universities.

Education was important to Bertha, but so was fairness. When her children were not allowed to swim at Barton Springs Pool or ice skate at the Ice Palace skating rink because they were Black, Bertha had enough. She made speeches and pressured local government to allow children of all races to use and enjoy Austin's recreation centers. She started the Mothers Action Council and led peaceful protests. Not only did she get Austin to integrate Barton Springs Pool and the Ice Palace, but ALL public facilities in Austin.

Bertha dedicated her life to opening up opportunities for the Black children and families of Austin. She earned many awards, but she was perhaps most proud of the Bertha Sadler Means Young Women's Leadership Academy being named in her honor.

DR. W. CHARLES AKINS

DR. W. CHARLES AKINS

Dr. William Charles Akins (1932–2017) was born and raised in East Austin, where he attended segregated schools, including Kealing Junior High and the old L. C. Anderson High School.

In 1964, after earning degrees from Huston-Tillotson College (now Huston-Tillotson University), Prairie View A&M College, and Southwest Texas State University, Charles became the first Black teacher at Johnston High School. He went on to become an assistant principal, and, in 1973, the first Black principal of the new L. C. Anderson High School.

This was when the Austin school district was trying to integrate more schools. They would bring kids from Black neighborhoods in East Austin to Anderson (a controversial practice called "bussing"). It was not an easy transition, and Charles would stand outside as the busses arrived to help keep the peace. Despite the difficulties, he said "I believe in inclusion. I really do. I think that's what being American is all about."

Charles was an incredible leader, and he led the way for all of Austin's schools to be successful, diverse, and offer every opportunity for students and teachers to shine. He was deeply honored when in 2000, W. Charles Akins High School first opened its doors.

DR. CHARLES E. URDY

Dr. Charles E. Urdy (b. 1933), an educator, scientist, and beloved community leader was born in Georgetown, Texas. The twelfth of thirteen children, young Charles worked the cotton fields with his family. It was hard, hot work and Charles made a promise that he was going to go to school because "I'm sure not going to be doing *this* for the rest of my life!" He kept that promise and in 1956 became one of the "Precursors," the first group of Black students to attend (newly integrated) UT at Austin. He then became one of "The Fabulous Five," a group of five Black UT students among the first to earn their PhDs in Chemistry.

After leaving UT, Charles taught at Prairie View A&M College, North Carolina College at Durham, and Huston-Tillotson College (now Huston-Tillotson University). He worked at the Lower Colorado River Authority, served as Mayor Pro Tem (someone who acts as mayor if the actual mayor is absent), and held an unmatched *five* terms on the Austin City Council! For all he's done to support Austin's Black community, especially in East Austin, the plaza at East 11th and Waller Streets—featuring a clocktower and *Rhapsody*, a mosaic depicting Austin musicians—was named in his honor.

DOROTHY TURNER

Dorothy Turner (1935–2005) was a fierce Civil Rights advocate for East Austin and the Black community. As a young woman, she rode the bus to west Austin to clean white families' homes. It was on these bus rides, while talking to other maids, that her political education started.

Years later, Dorothy created *Grassroots Struggle*, a newspaper dedicated to printing stories about "the help"—people who didn't have much of a voice, and whose stories were not being told. Throughout the 1980s, *Grassroots Struggle* boldly reported stories about Black people and East Austin. But Dorothy was only getting started!

Dorothy was also a force for change. She pressured Austin city officials to hire more Black managers—including Austin's first female assistant city manager and first African American personnel director. She also played an important role in establishing the Millennium Youth Entertainment Complex.

Known as "Mrs. T," Dorothy—alongside Velma Roberts—cofounded the Black Citizens Task Force. This organization fought issues of discrimination and unfair treatment in the Black community. Once again, Dorothy worked hard to make sure every voice was heard in the fight for a fair and equal community.

In 2008, the Turner-Roberts Recreation Center opened in East Austin, named in honor of Dorothy Turner's enduring impact and inspiring legacy.

ERNIE MAE MILLER

Ernie Mae Miller (1927–2010) was a beloved figure and a talented blues and jazz musician with a career spanning over half a century! Born in Austin in 1927, Ernie Mae learned to play the piano by ear at a very young age. She often listened to her grandmother's records on an old Victrola for hours, which inspired her love of music.

As a student at Anderson High School (named for her grandfather, L.C. Anderson), Ernie Mae switched to playing the saxophone, as the school didn't need a piano player. She loved music so much, she used to sneak out of her house to watch big stars like Count Basie or Duke Ellington when they were passing through town.

During World War II, Ernie Mae played the saxophone in the Prairie View Co-eds, an African American all-girl swing band from Prairie View Normal and Industrial College that toured the country. As a pianist, Ernie Mae became famous in the early 1950s with a long-running gig at the New Orleans Club on Red River Street, playing jazz and even "The Eyes of Texas" on game days. She was inducted into the Austin Music Hall of Fame in 2007. Ernie Mae also played at many of Austin's best hotel lounges and restaurants, as well as now-gone clubs like the Flamingo Lounge, the Jade Room, and the Commodore Perry Hotel, where she left an amazing mark on Austin's rich music history.

DR. EVERETT H. GIVENS

Dr. Everett Givens (1888–1962) is known as one of Austin's first Black dentists. But he is legendary for his fight for fair treatment of Austin's Black citizens.

Born in Austin in 1888, Everett went on to serve in World War I. He continued his education when he returned home, studying dentistry. This is where his fight for Civil Rights began.

Back before Everett was born, in 1882, Texas approved funding for a Black university in Austin. But it was never built. Fast forward to 1946, when Everett was prevented from taking a dental course at University of Texas, which was segregated. Everett went to court, saying Texas violated its constitution by not providing space for him to continue his studies.

That was just the beginning for Everett. He rallied for better streets, better parks, improved bus services, bridges connecting East Austin to the center of the city, and more. He pushed for fair treatment from the Austin police, and for the department to hire more Black deputies. And he was instrumental in Austin hiring its first Black firefighters.

Everett's efforts and inspiration are still felt today. He's been honored in many ways, including having the Givens Park in East Austin named for him.

GENE RAMEY

Eugene (Gene) Glasco Ramey (1913–1984) was a jazz bassist born in Austin just before World War I. His grandmother, Glasco, formerly enslaved, came from Madagascar and shared rich musical traditions with her family. Gene's family was full of music lovers: his grandfather played the violin, his father strummed the banjo, his mother played the organ, and his brother sang.

In 1931, after learning to play the trumpet and baritone, Gene graduated from L.C. Anderson High School—the only school in Austin where Black students could obtain a high school diploma during many years of segregation.

Gene's love of music led him to Kansas City, where he studied under jazz pioneer Walter Page and learned to play the double bass. During the 1930s and 1940s, Kansas City was a jazz music hotspot and some say the birthplace of bebop—a free and more improvised form of jazz. Gene joined Jay McShann's orchestra and became a beloved part of the swing jazz scene.

In 1944, he moved to New York City, where he played with famous jazz musicians like Miles Davis, Thelonius Monk, and Charlie "Bird" Parker. He even played all over Europe with Thelonius Monk's trio, creating his unique bebop sound.

In 1976, Gene returned to Austin as a "living legend" and mentored young musicians until he passed away on December 8, 1984. Today, his music still lives on, inspiring jazz lovers of all ages.

J. MASON BREWER

Scholar and folklorist **John Mason Brewer** (1896–1975) was born in Goliad, Texas, in 1896, surrounded by stories. Mason's grandfathers were wagoners who drove across Texas. His father worked many jobs and was once a cowboy. The stories they shared lit up Mason's imagination and fostered a love of folktales, especially about his home state. Mason's mother was a schoolteacher, and she made sure he had plenty of books to grow his love of reading and learning.

When Mason graduated from Wiley College in 1917, he worked as a teacher and wrote poetry. He also collected the folktales he heard at schools and churches and barbershops—the places where Black Texans lived and worked.

In the 1930s, Mason shared some of his folktales with folklorist J. Frank Dobie. Dobie was impressed with Mason's work and helped publish his stories in a collection called "Juneteenth." Many books followed, filled with tales of hardship and humor from Texas's former slaves and their descendants.

J. Mason Brewer became the first African American member of the Texas Folklore Society and the Texas Institute of Letters. Over his fifty-year career, Mason almost single-handedly preserved the African American folklore of his home state.

DR. JOHN L. WARFIELD

Dr. John L. Warfield (1936–2007) (fondly called "Doc" by many of his students, colleagues, and friends within the Black Austin community) was an incredible teacher, scholar, activist, psychologist, and Civil Rights visionary who made a big impact on the UT campus and beyond!

A teacher at the University of Texas at Austin for twenty-six years, Doc brought together two important centers: one for African American Studies and the other for African and African American Research. Doc became the first director of the new center and played a crucial role in shaping its faculty, classes, and research. He worked hard to build connections between the academic world and the outside Black community of Austin. He even founded Community Radio, Inc., which runs KAZI-FM, Austin's community-based radio station.

Doc cared a lot about activism and social change. He wrote about the role of race and academics in college sports before many people were talking about it. In 2000, the Center for African and African American Studies even created a special scholarship in Doc's name—the John L. Warfield Undergraduate Research Scholarship—which encourages undergraduate students to conduct research about Africa and the African diaspora.

DR. JOHN QUILL TAYLOR KING, SR.

Dr. John Quill Taylor King, Sr. (1921–2011) was an influential educator in Austin. Born in Memphis, Tennessee, his family moved to Austin in 1925 and opened King Funeral Home. John was an excellent student and graduated from high school early. He went on to get a math degree at Fisk University in Nashville, Tennessee, before joining the Army in 1941. He served in the Pacific during World War II, and then he returned home to continue his education.

While John got his masters and PhD in mathematics, he kept his connection to the Army by joining the Army Reserve. He served as a reservist for more than thirty years.

In 1947, John began teaching mathematics at Huston-Tillotson College (now Huston-Tillotson University). He was a much-loved teacher and administrator, and in 1965, he became president of the college, a position he held until 1988! He is the longest-serving president in Huston-Tillotson history. John always supported his students and faculty, and he was part of dozens of organizations that supported the communities he loved. He was tireless in his desire to help people achieve their goals.

JOHNNY HOLMES

Johnny Holmes (1917–2001) is the visionary behind Victory Grill Cafe, who some say kick-started Austin's famous music scene. Johnny opened Victory Grill on September 2, 1945, which is Victory Over Japan Day (or V-J Day). It was the day the government of Japan surrendered, ending World War II.

Austin was still segregated at that time, and Johnny wanted Victory Grill to be a place where Black soldiers returning from the war could come for a cold drink and a hot meal. In the 1940s and 1950s, Victory Grill became a favorite spot for amazing R&B and blues musicians to perform, marking the very beginning of Austin's fame as a great city for music. Legendary musicians lit up the stage here, including B.B. King, Clarence "Gatemouth" Brown, Billie Holliday, Chuck Berry, and Ike and Tina Turner.

Victory Grill—and its neighborhood—suffered in the 1970s and 80s, but eventually, friends and neighbors brought it back to life. Today, the Historic Victory Grill is known for its fried chicken and waffles, and is listed on the National Register of Historic Places. Johnny Holmes opened a cafe for the Black community to gather. But he also created an important landmark in the growth of a truly American music tradition.

REVEREND LEE LEWIS CAMPBELL

Lee Lewis Campbell (1866–1927) was born in Milam County, Texas, in 1866. Growing up, he attended a small school with only one teacher for all the students. By the time he was fifteen or sixteen years old, Campbell was helping teach his fellow students. He was a natural teacher—and student—and went on to attend Bishop College in Marshall and then University of Chicago.

Lee returned to Texas in 1887, married Ella Williams, and started a family. He continued to teach and became a Baptist minister. In 1892, he became pastor of Ebenezer Baptist Church in Austin. He remained pastor for thirty-five years, and led many organizations that helped the African American community in Austin.

He founded St. John's Institute and Orphanage and served as president of the General Baptist State Convention in Texas. In 1889, he founded the *Austin Herald*, a newspaper published every Saturday.

Lee was also president of St. John's Colored Association Encampment, an annual event where thousands of African American people came to Austin to discuss race relations. His funeral in 1927 was attended by more than 5,000 people. In 1939, L.L. Campbell Elementary School in Austin was named in his honor.

MARY AGNES YERWOOD THOMPSON

Mary Agnes Yerwood Thompson (1911–2001) was born in Austin in 1911. She was a leader in education and women's services, and earned two master's degrees from the University of Texas at Austin.

In 1933, at the age of twenty-two, she founded a much-needed nursery school in East Austin. It was known as the Howson Child Development Laboratory, and was the first nursery school in the area.

Almost thirty years later, in 1960, Mary helped establish the Austin chapter of the Links, a national organization dedicated to creating community among African American women. In 1995, Mary was inducted into the National Women's Hall of Fame for her work and outstanding service to the women's community of Austin. A lifelong member of the American Association of University Women (Austin), Mary died on September 9, 2001, at the age of ninety.

MARY FRANCES FREEMAN BAYLOR

Mary Frances Freeman Baylor (1929–1997) was born in 1929 in a west Austin freedmen community that her ancestors had established in the 1870s. (A freedmen community was a neighborhood established by freed slaves.) That community became Clarksville.

Clarksville was isolated, and its public services—roads, sanitation, hospitals, and schools—were badly in need of funding and repair. Mary became Clarksville's biggest champion.

In the 1960s, Mary volunteered in President Johnson's War on Poverty program. She later became director of the Clarksville Neighborhood Center. The center was an important resource for Clarksville's residents, helping people find jobs, housing, counseling services, youth programs, and more.

In the late 1960s, Mary protested against the construction of Texas Loop 1, a highway (also called MoPac Expressway) that would destroy hundreds of Clarksville homes. The highway was built, but not before Mary helped secure more than $1 million to build a community center and playground and to improve Clarksville's public services.

In 1978, Mary founded the Clarksville Community Development Corporation (CCDC) to preserve the history of Clarksville and ensure affordable housing. After she passed away in 1997, the Texas Legislature commemorated her achievements and the city of Austin named a park in her honor.

MARY JANE SIMS

Mary Jane Sims (1874–1950), born in Round Rock, Texas, in 1874, was an exceptional teacher, writer, and composer, best known for dedicating her life to children and literacy in Austin's Black community. She began her teaching career at sixteen, teaching Black children in Bastrop County. She later taught in Galveston and at Prairie View State Normal School while writing children's books and creating music.

After graduating from college in 1927, Mary Jane continued teaching in Austin, playing a very important role in education for Black elementary students. In 1942, she authored two children's books, *Carlo* and *Mule-Eared Bunny*. She moved to California in 1943, returning to Austin in 1946, where she founded the first nursery school for African American children.

Mary Jane's dedication to education and her community left a lasting legacy. In her honor, the Austin Education Association established the Mary Jane Sims Scholarship in 1956. An East Austin elementary school was named after her to celebrate her remarkable contributions to children's education.

NORMAN WILFRED SCALES, SR.

Norman Wilfred Scales, Sr. (1918–1981) was born on November 11, 1918, in Hillsboro, Texas. He grew up in Austin, but during the summers, Norman's family picked cotton on farms in Northern and Central Texas.

In 1936, Norman graduated from high school and enrolled at Tillotson College (now Huston-Tillotson University)—a Historically Black College and University (HBCU).

In 1940, as WWII was raging in Europe, Norman joined the Army Air Corps, which, like the rest of the country, was segregated. Norman was smart and hardworking, and was stationed in Tuskegee, Alabama, the only airfield open to Black pilots. The men there were known as the Tuskegee Airmen. The Black airmen often felt they had to work harder to prove to their white superiors that they were brave and worthy. And work hard they did! The Tuskegee Airmen became an elite group of fighters, known for their skill and bravery.

During the war, Norman flew more than seventy missions over enemy territory and survived a plane crash. After the war ended, Norman was one of 150 Tuskegee Airmen awarded the Distinguished Flying Cross in recognition of his combat service.

RICHARD ARVIN OVERTON

Richard Arvin Overton (1906–2018) had an extraordinary (and extraordinarily long) life. Born in 1906 in Bastrop County, Texas, Richard lived to be 112 years old. This makes him a 'supercentenarian', which is a person over 110 years old! In fact, at the time of his death, Richard was America's oldest World War II veteran and the oldest man in the United States.

The grandson of enslaved people, Richard lived through many of America's most historic events, including the Great Depression, two World Wars, and the Civil Rights Movement. After joining the Army in 1941, Richard served in the all-Black 1887th Engineer Aviation Battalion and was stationed in Hawaii within days of the attack on Pearl Harbor. He also fought in some of World War II's toughest battles in Iwo Jima and Okinawa, Japan.

In 2013, President Obama honored Richard during a special Veterans Day ceremony. The next year, Austin Community College awarded Richard an honorary degree for his century of many achievements. In 2017, the Austin City Council gave Hamilton Avenue—where Richard lived for more than seventy years—the honorary name "Richard Overton Avenue." He even went viral—with more than forty million views—after sharing his secrets to a long and happy life: whiskey, cigars, and butter pecan ice cream!

SELENA CASH

Selena Cash (1928–2019) was a groundbreaking educator in Austin, leaving a lasting impression on the lives of thousands of Austin students.

Born in Pelham, Texas, Selena was descended from former slaves who established one of the first freedmen colonies in central Texas. Selena went to public school in Forth Worth, before earning her first degree from Huston-Tillotson College (now Huston-Tillotson University). She continued her studies at Texas Southern University, UT Austin, and Prairie View A&M University.

Selena became a teacher in Austin, and eventually, she became the Austin Independent School District's first Black female principal at Murchison Junior High School. She believed that all students had gifts and could succeed—even if they didn't go to college. In all the schools she led, Selena tried to establish classes that would teach kids life skills and train them to be chefs, woodworkers, mechanics, plumbers, and more.

After she retired from teaching, Selena continued to support her community at Midtown Live, a sports cafe that brought people together. Forever supporting the people around her, the Austin community knew Selena as Mama Cash.

VELMA ROBERTS

Velma Roberts (1930-2000) was a single mom on welfare when, in 1968, she met a group of students from University of Texas School of Social Work. They wanted to find a local recipient of public assistance to become president of the Welfare Rights Organization (WRO). Velma was the only one who said yes. She spent the rest of her life fighting for people—especially women and single moms—who lived in poverty.

Velma began going to city council meetings. She was never afraid to stand up and fight for poor Black and Latino families who were often ignored during the 1960s and 70s. She fought for free breakfast and lunch at Austin schools and access to free childcare for working moms. She worked with the local police to stop the unfair harassment of Black and brown citizens. She helped East Austin's poor families get easier access to food banks.

Together with activist Dorothy Turner, Velma led the Black Citizen's Task Force and cofounded a local newspaper, *Grassroots Struggle*. They fought to have city organizations hire more Black managers, and to build more recreation centers for Austin's Black students.

Velma had her hand in dozens of efforts to make life better for all of Austin's Black families, a legacy that carries on today.

WILLIE MAE KIRK

Willie Mae Kirk (1921–2013) believed that "if you have anything at all, you have something to share." And share she did. Willie Mae—also known as "Ankie"—shared her time, energy, and kindness with the Austin community for decades.

Born in Manor, Texas, Willie Mae was one of thirteen children. She grew up to be a teacher in Austin. She taught for more than thirty-two years!

Along with teaching, Willie Mae served on the Austin Library Commission for more than ten years. With Ada Anderson, she helped start the Austin chapter of the Jack and Jill Foundation, which helped local children. She was active in the Civil Rights Movement, protesting segregation in schools, at lunch counters, and at Barton Springs, where Black families—including her own—were not allowed to swim. Willie Mae made sure her children understood the importance of fighting for what's right and working hard for your community. Her son, Ron Kirk, became Dallas's first-ever African American mayor and then served in President Obama's cabinet.

In 2012, the Oak Springs Library was renamed to honor Willie Mae Kirk. She died the following year, at age 92.

WILLIE RAY DAVIS

Willie Ray Davis (1924–2006) grew up in a segregated Texas. In the 1940s, he joined the Navy and served in WWII. When he returned, he married his high school sweetheart and started a family.

In 1952, Willie Ray looked to one of his heroes, hall-of-fame baseball player Jackie Robinson. Robinson had become the first Black player to join a Major League Baseball team (in 1947), breaking the so-called "color barrier." Inspired, Willie Ray became one of the first Black men to join the Austin Fire Department.

Willie Ray was assigned to Old Fire Station 5 at 1005 Lydia Street in East Austin. His success inspired others so much that by 1954, African Americans were hired as firefighters in Houston, San Antonio, Dallas, and other Texas cities. In 1966, Willie Ray was promoted to lieutenant, becoming the first African American fire officer in Texas. In 1969, he was named Austin Firefighter of the Year. Then, in 1973, Willie Ray was promoted to captain.

Recognized for his exceptional technical knowledge in the field of fire prevention and containment, Willie Ray joined the department's public education division. He retired with honors in 1983 and received the Distinguished Service Award.

WILLIE WELLS

American sports hero **Willie (the Devil) Wells** (1905–1989) wasn't just any athlete—he was a super athlete! Born in Austin in 1905, Willie was a star baseball and football player in high school and went on to play professional baseball in 1923. The Major Leagues were segregated at the time, so Willie played in the Negro Leagues.

His first team was the Austin Black Senators. Willie was so talented that some called him the greatest living baseball player not in the National Baseball Hall of Fame! (Willie earned his rightful place in the Hall of Fame in 1997.)

Considered the best Black shortstop of his time, Willie played for many teams in the Negro Leagues from 1924–1948. Lightning fast, a powerhouse at bat, and a wizard with his glove, it seemed there was nothing Willie couldn't do—and no ball he couldn't catch!

He also improved game safety by being the first player in history to use a batting helmet after suffering a concussion during a game against the Newark Eagles. Willie even shared his baseball wisdom with none other than the legendary Jackie Robinson, teaching him the art of the double play. Talk about a game changer and historymaker!

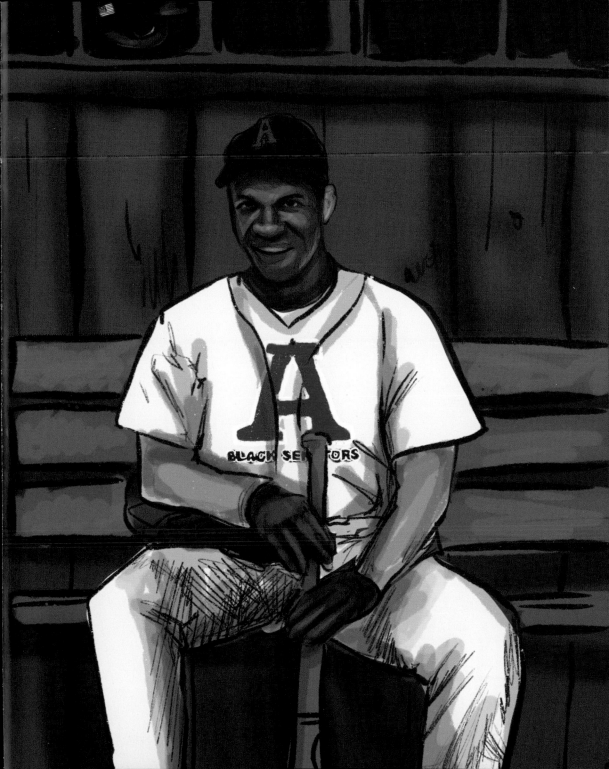

A NOTE TO READERS

This project is a collaboration between the Black Leaders Collective; the George Washington Carver Museum, Cultural and Genealogy Center; and visual artist Sadé Lawson. The goal of this partnership is to develop a children's book that honors African American trailblazers who played a critical role in the development of Black Austin's social, political, and cultural heritage. This endeavor is about educating youth and influencing an emerging generation of Black leaders who understand the legacy of community-based organizing for racial and economic justice. Through this work, we seek to resurrect, share, and inspire a deeper understanding of this place we call Austin, while honoring the people who helped build this city.

ACKNOWLEDGMENTS

This book goes out to the leaders, dreamers, risk-takers, innovators . . . the people's champs. May you continue to be a bright light in this world and a beacon of love in all that you do.

Our sincerest gratitude to the family and friends of the changemakers celebrated in this series. You carry the torch and preserve the legacies of giants. We hope we helped you archive their invaluable contributions to our community for generations to come.

To the Black Leaders Collective, we did it! We set out to creatively preserve the history of our city and the brilliance of the leaders that built it. Mission Accomplished x 10.

Elle Mitchell, you are the reason we turned this initiative into a children's book. Watching you light up and learn (me too!) when we read fun books together led me and the team to realize the incredible impact colorful images and interesting stories make on readers of all ages. Now the book will be published just in time for you to read it to your baby brother, Pierre Mitchell. How sweet is that!? Thank you, sweet babies, for being my daily inspiration.

And finally, to our phenomenal team at Arcadia Children's Books, the outpouring of love and dedication is beyond describable. You understood our vision from the jump and have worked tirelessly to elevate us in ways we couldn't imagine. We are grateful for your trust, for your guidance, and for your partnership.

CONTRIBUTORS AND SPONSORS

Terry P. Mitchell prides herself in being the founder of the Black Leaders Collective (in areas of social impact, DEI, and policy reform), founding cochair of The Black Fund (a giving network for Black organizations), cofounder and COO of E & Co Tech (a software and mobile development firm), and cofounder and CEO of Glam Beauty Bar (a hair and aesthetics salon). She is also the co-owner of *Austin Woman Magazine*, cochair of the Black Fund at Austin Community Foundation, and Commissioner for City of Austin Small and Minority Business Resources department.

Her faith, quick wit, and unwavering determination to succeed has propelled her to levels beyond her imagination. As a native of the music capital of the world—Austin, Texas—and a first-generation descendant from Trinidad and Tobago, Terry has cultivated a sincere adoration for travel, culture, and diversity. Terry graduated from the University of Texas at Austin with a bachelor's degree in Corporate Communications and a certification in Business Foundations.

Carre Adams is the chief curator and director of the George Washington Carver Museum, Cultural and Genealogy Center in Austin, Texas—an institution dedicated to the collection, preservation, and exhibition of Black material culture.

In addition to his curatorial practice, he is also an artistic director, mixed-media artist, filmmaker, and music producer. His creative work explores love, sovereignty, and inheritance. His projects have been featured on Arts in

Context produced by PBS; Feministing; *Glasstire*: Texas Visual Art News & Reviews; Art in America; Sightlines; and *Forbes*.

A former codirector at allgo, a statewide LGBTQIA + BIPOC arts and justice organization, he has repeatedly sought professional opportunities that allow him to align his creative pursuits with movements for racial equity and justice.

He received his B.A. from Sarah Lawrence College in visual arts and African and African diaspora studies.

Sadé Lawson, based in Austin, TX, is a dynamic artist known for her vibrant and empowering artworks. Specializing in portraiture, landscapes, and the fusion of colors, she crafts personalized symbolic stories that resonate with viewers. As a muralist, visual artist, and licensed nail technician, Sadé's creativity extends beyond traditional boundaries. Her unconventional combination of skills reflects in both large-scale murals and intricate nail art. Rooted in Austin's diverse energy, Sadé's creations not only tell her personal story, but also uplift the moods of those who engage with her eclectic and empowering body of work.

George Washington Carver Museum, Cultural and Genealogy Center

Through the preservation and exhibition of African American material culture, history, and aesthetic expression, the Carver Museum works to create a space where the global contributions of all Black people are celebrated. We accomplish this by telling stories about our local community and connecting those histories to larger narratives about Blackness.

Founded in 1980, the museum serves as a cultural anchor, hosting exhibits, performances, and public programs that center the culture and history of Black people.

Black Leaders Collective

The Black Leaders Collective (BLC) is a collaboration of Central-Texas leaders representing grassroots community members, nonprofit leaders, entrepreneurs, artists, activists, educators, policymakers, and young professionals.

BLC is leading a transformative movement that is intersectional and intergenerational. We are creating a mechanism for change that is Black conceived and Black led to define the priorities of the Black diaspora in Central Texas.

Because we know it is our responsibility as Black leaders in the Black community to identify and solve issues that affect us today and in our future, the Black Leaders Collective has united more than one hundred Black leaders to envision and execute a seven-generational sustainability plan in the areas of health, education, housing, arts, and economic and workforce development.

Visit us at www.blackleaderscollectiveglobal.org